PRAYER *Journal*

Presented to: _____

From: _____

Date: _____

Copyright © 2019 Phyllis Thomas

All rights reserved under the international copyright law. No part of this book may be reproduced or transmitted in any form or by any means, electronic or mechanical, including photocopying, recording, or by any information storage and retrieval system, without the express, written permission of the publisher or the author. The exception is reviewers, who may quote brief passages in a review.

ISBN 9781562293772

Christian Living Books, Inc.
P. O. Box 7584
Largo, MD 20792
christianlivingbooks.com
We bring your dreams to fruition.

Printed in the United States of America.

HOW TO USE THIS BOOK

This prayer journal is designed to help you make prayer, Bible reading, fasting, and witnessing for Christ a lifestyle. These are important tools that will keep your soul spiritually nourished and equipped. They will help you maintain a close and refreshing relationship with God.

You will participate in a series of activities that will develop good habits in your life. Every repetitive action becomes a habit, and good habits are hard to break. Strive to be addicted to God and His righteousness.

Each day, read the scripture and inspirational thought of the month. Allow them to guide your meditation and devotions. Pray the monthly prayer aloud and complete the monthly challenge.

Read the morning and evening scripture each day. Mark the box with a ✓ once you have completed the daily reading. Stay consistent in reading the daily scriptures and within a year you will have read the entire Bible.

The Daily Checklist is a built-in accountability section. After answering the six questions each day, check off the box. Then, keep a record of answered prayers on pages 93-95.

I challenge you to begin your journey today. You will not regret committing yourself to make God your first priority. Enjoy this spiritual journey with God.

CONTENTS

A – Z Affirmations and Prayers iv

January: The Importance of Prayer. 9

February: The Importance of God's Word 16

March: The Importance of Fasting. 23

April: Have Faith in God 30

May: Fulfilling the Purpose of God 37

June: Blessed for Service. 44

July: Appointed to be Anointed 51

August: Walk in your Deliverance 58

September: Living a Victorious Life in God. 65

October: God's Favor. 72

November: God's Divine Will 79

December: God's Gift of Love 86

Answered Prayer Chart. 93

A – Z AFFIRMATIONS AND PRAYERS

A – AVAILABLE Lord, I am available to You. I give You all of me, not just a part, as a living sacrifice to be used for Your glory.

Heavenly Father, You have always covered me with Your love and given me the best in life. Now I stand ready to give myself totally to You. I am available to You, Lord; every part of me is for Your service. In Jesus Christ's name. Amen.

B – BLESSED I am blessed with the blessings from God's heavenly treasures in every area of my life. It is because of God's precious and unfailing promises that I can and will declare, "I am blessed!"

Gracious heavenly Father, almighty King, I give You praise for all Your manifold blessings toward me. I bless Your name for all Your benefits. I give You thanks for the opportunity to lift You up in the beauty of holiness. Thank You for Your provision, protection, joy, peace, faith, strength, love, kindness, and all the heavenly abundance You send my way. Thank You, Lord. Amen.

C – COMMITMENT I commit my mind, body, soul, and spirit to God. I will stay committed to God and trust Him. With my commitment, I will receive His choice blessings.

Dear Lord, it is because of You that I live, move, and have my being. Lord, this day, I commit myself to You. Please lead and guide me during this journey of life so that I will not fail You. Thank You for Your faithfulness, care, and concern for me. I am grateful You chose me to be a part of You. I praise You, Lord. Amen.

D – DELIGHT God, I delight to do Thy will and become who You want me to be. My heart's longing is for Your desire to be my desire. With this harmonious connection, I will be more than a conqueror through You.

Awesome Savior, King of kings and Lord of lords, my desire is to please You from the moment I wake up until the time I close my eyes. I am delighted that because of Your grace and mercy, I have the opportunity to receive the overshadowing of Your presence any hour, minute, or second of the day I reach out to You. Keep me in the center of Your heart's desire, and I will delight myself in Thee. I love You, Lord, forever! Amen.

E – ENDEAVOR I will not fail in my efforts. I will succeed according to Your divine plan, purpose, and will for my life. I endeavor to follow Your directions for me so that I can stay free in You.

Heavenly Father, I thank You for never giving up on me. I am determined to walk in Your will by taking heed to Your wise counsel given to me in Your Word. I endeavor to be watchful in all that I say and do in order to please You. I thank You, Lord, for giving me another chance to serve You. Amen.

F – FOCUS There is nothing that God will not do for me if I keep my focus on Him and totally trust Him.

My Savior, You are the center of my joy. You are the sunlight in my life and the air that I breathe. Lord, I look to You for help. There is no other help like Yours. Lord, I want to be close to You. Draw me closer to You. I know being close to You will help me stay focused on You, my satisfaction guaranteed. My goal is to be fixed on Christ's unlimited supply of blessings. Thank You for being my supplier. Amen.

G – GREATNESS I serve a great God; therefore, I am destined for greatness. My destiny for greatness in God is by choice, not by chance.

Dear heavenly Savior, You are my omnipotent, almighty, majestic, and magnificent Lord. The greatness of Your character and the attributes of Your personality are to be adored, exalted, magnified, and appreciated. Thank You, Lord, for dwelling in me. Now I will press forward toward my destiny of greatness. In Jesus' name. Amen.

H – HOPE I will keep hope alive, for without hope there is no future for me. I will continually hope for what I do not see. With patience, I will wait for the manifestation of God's promises to me.

Sovereign God, You are my hope in this life and the life to come. Strengthen my faith in You. I realize that without hope in You, I would be as a drifter on a wavy sea. Lord, I depend on You. You are in control of all things pertaining to me. Thank You for the hope I have in You. Lord, You are my source of everlasting life. Thank You, Jesus. Amen.

I – IDENTITY I thank God for my identity, for who I am. I know who I am, for God created me to be who I am in the likeness of His image. My identity will not be tainted with the things of this world.

Dear Lord, thank You for making me in Your image and likeness. Help me to maintain a godly identity so the devil will not steal or destroy who I am in You. Lord, continue to mold and shape me for Your service. Thank You for my identity in You. You are an awesome God! Amen.

J – JOY The joy of the Lord is my strength. The joy that I have surpasses any superficial joy given by the world. The joy I have is the reality of who lives in me.

Heavenly Father, thank You for the fruit of the Spirit – JOY. Lord, let Your joy continue to abide in me even in the midst of apparent turmoil and trouble. Keep me strengthened with that unspeakable and refreshing JOY (Just One You). Amen.

K – KINGDOM I will obey the Scriptures and seek first the kingdom of God and His righteousness. Then I will receive all the things God has for me.

Lord Jesus, thank You for providing me with the keys to Your kingdom. Your Word tells me that whatsoever I bind on earth, it shall be bound in heaven, and whatsoever I loose on earth shall be loosed in heaven. Thank You, Lord, for giving me the kingdom keys of power. Thank You, Lord, for kingdom authority. Amen.

L - LOVE I will daily renew my vow to God to love Him with all my heart, soul, mind, and strength. God is the love of my life.

Dear Jesus, thank You for Your unconditional love for me. It is because of Your unselfish love that You died on the cross and rose from the grave to cover my sinful soul. Lord, I appreciate You loving me the way You do. I realize no one in this world can provide such an unfailing and pure love like You. Lord, thank You for being my essence of love. You are and always will be the love of my life. Amen.

M – MERCY I'm blessed with the mercies of God. His mercy walks with me daily.

Dear Jesus, thank You for Your favor of mercy. It is because of Your mercy that I have not been consumed. I thank You that Your compassion toward me does not fail. Thank You for renewing Your mercy and grace to me every morning. I'm grateful for Your faithfulness that always abounds toward me. Great is Your love and kindness. Amen.

N – NUMINOUS I am expecting a supernatural miracle every day. I will experience God's numinous presence as I submit my all to Him. Nothing is impossible for God.

Dear Jesus, I ask You to cover me with Your Spirit and saturate me with Your numinous anointing. Lord, take me in Your spiritual elevator to the level You desire me to go. I want to grow spiritually and become a spiritual giant in You. My desire is for Your supernatural power to work through me continually. Do it, Lord. In Jesus' name, I pray. Amen.

O – OVERFLOW My life is totally fulfilled as I walk in the overflow of God's abundance.

Dear Lord, keep me living in the overflow of Your love, joy, peace, faith, mercy, strength, power, anointing, healing, patience, kindness, gentleness, meekness, and temperance. I thank You for the overflow of Your Spirit. Lord, keep me filled and thrilled with Your presence. Thank You, Lord, for the opportunity to experience spiritual freedom while living in the overflow of Your grace. Amen.

P – POWER God has given me the power to stand and go through tests; I know I'll make it because with God on my side, I have the best.

Dear Lord, thank You for Your magnificent power. I realize that all power belongs to You. Engulf me with Your divine power. Teach me how to use this power to combat the devil. Lord, You said in

Your Word that I have power over all the power of the enemy. So thank You, Lord, for keeping me walking in Your power continually. Amen.

Q – QUIETNESS In quietness, there is confidence and strength. I will study to be quiet and learn by listening with intensity.

Heavenly Father, bridle my tongue; put a bit in my mouth. Let my words be few and seasoned with Your grace. Help me to study to be quiet and do my own business. Lord, I thank You right now for teaching me that in quietness I will gain confidence and strength in You. Lord, help me to respond with a soft answer and a meek, quiet spirit. Let the words of my mouth, as well as the meditation and quietness of my heart, be acceptable in Thy sight. Amen.

R – REJOICE I will rejoice in God for choosing me to be a representative for Him. I will rejoice in the up times and in the down times, for praise is what I do.

Lord Jesus, I rejoice in You for all You have done for, in, and through me. Let Your praises be carved on my lips and joy bells ring out on the inside. I will praise You because praise is natural for the upright. I'm glad to be a part of You, for You are royalty! I will rejoice and sing praises unto You my Majesty and my King. Amen.

S – SPEAK That which I speak will come to pass. I will not allow the doubt in my mind to last. I believe in God's promises because He is a man of His word. I will totally trust Him and not be detoured.

Lord Jesus, Your Word says that a man's belly shall be satisfied with the fruit of his mouth and with the increase of his lips shall he be filled. Lord, keep my spirit filled with the fruits of love, joy, peace, goodness, and kindness. Keep the positive thoughts of You flowing through me. I know that death and life are in the power of what I speak; therefore, I will speak life abundantly. Thank You, Lord, for blessing me with a mouthpiece of praise, worship, and thanksgiving. Amen.

T- TRANSFORMED I will not conform to this world's standards, but I will continually be transformed in my thoughts, actions, and speech. I will strive to maintain my spiritual transformation in all that I say and do to be acceptable to God.

Savior, it is my endeavor to please You in all that I do. Daily keep my mind renewed with the things of You. Keep my heart pure at all times. Keep me transformed so that I will always project Your characteristics. Thank You, Lord, for rescuing me from a world of sin and transforming my life. I appreciate You dwelling in me and giving me the desire not to compromise my salvation. Thank You, Lord, for a permanent transformation. Amen.

U – UNLIMITED I have access to an unlimited supply of God's blessings. I will walk in the abundance of God's abilities and resources. There are no limits to God's blessings for me.

Jesus, I love You! Thank You for being a God of provision with no limits to Your power, anointing, healing, deliverance, resources, and blessings. I receive the unlimited miracles You have just for me.

Lord, I will not doubt You or restrict Your ability to move in my life. I receive the boundless flow of You in and through me. Amen.

V – VALUE I value my relationship with God; therefore, I will seek Him daily for guidance and strength on this journey called life. I am a valuable asset to the kingdom of God.

Dear heavenly Father, please help me to always be an asset to You and others. Lord, I do not ever want to be a liability because liabilities have no worth, but assets can be priceless. I want to be a vessel of value and honor. Teach me to understand my worth in You. Lord, I value Your love toward me. Please keep me as the apple of Your eye. Amen.

W – WISDOM I will apply the knowledge of God to gain wisdom from Him. God's wisdom is more precious than silver or gold.

Lord Jesus, You said in Your Word that if we lack wisdom, we should ask, and You will give it liberally. Lord, crown my head with the wisdom and knowledge of You and Your will for me. Replace my wisdom with Your wisdom and my understanding with Your understanding. Keep my thoughts elevated toward You. Let the words of Your wisdom impart my lips. Thank You, Lord, for wisdom. Amen.

X – X'D I endeavor daily to keep the devil "X'd" out of all areas of my life. I will insert God in every segment of my life.

Master, You are the love of my life and the sovereign God of my soul. Lord, I am trusting You to give me the strength, courage, and endurance to combat the devil daily. Lord, the devil has no room, say, or power in me. I have voluntarily "X'd" him out of all aspects of my life. As I submit myself to You, I will resist the devil (X him out), and he will flee in the name of Jesus. Thank You, Lord, for the victory and the power to put the devil under my feet. Amen.

Y – YIELD I will not yield to temptation. I will yield myself in humble submission to the master plan of God by giving Him a complete yes!

Dear Jesus, I give You my heart, mind, body, soul, and spirit. Every part of me I yield to You as an instrument for Your service. Lord, I will not yield to the devil to be defeated by him. I'm determined to be a yielding vessel fit for Your kingdom. I love You, Jesus, with all my heart. Amen.

Z – ZEST The ultimate zest for me is to keep the flavor of life in step with Christ.

Lord, You are my zest in life. Thank You, Father, for performing Your promises to me. I love experiencing Your flavor of goodness, grace, and kindness toward me. You are the one who keeps my life full of enjoyment. May the fragrance of You continue to disperse through me so that others will want to follow and be drawn to You. Lord, keep me in step and filled with Your zest. In Jesus' name. Amen.

January
THE IMPORTANCE OF PRAYER

 Scripture of the Month

"Pray without ceasing" (1 Thessalonians 5:17).

 Inspirational Thought

Ultimate relief and the abundance of peace are received through daily prayer.

 Prayer for the Month – Pray these personal prayers aloud

Dear Lord, it is such a pleasure and benefit to commune with You. This month, Lord, teach me the importance of prayer. Teach me how to pray and seek You with my whole heart, soul, mind, and spirit. Help me to understand that You want me to communicate with You, and You want to communicate with me. Now, Lord Jesus, take my mind and renew it. Take my heart; tenderize and refresh it. Take my soul and spirit; saturate them with Your presence. Lord, I look forward to receiving an outpouring of Your grace, mercy, and Spirit. I will forever give You praise, honor, and glory. In Jesus' name, I pray. Amen!

 Monthly Challenge

Pray a minimum of 15 minutes each day without interruptions. Prayer is the key to building your relationship with God.

 Daily Checklist

Each day, answer the six questions. Once you have answered them, place a checkmark in the box on the Daily Checklist chart.

1. Did you pray today?
2. Did you read a scripture(s)?
3. Did you pray for someone? Who?
4. Did you fast today?
5. Did you witness to someone about Jesus?
6. What did you receive from the Lord today?

DAILY CHECKLIST	Day 1	Day 2	Day 3	Day 4	Day 5	Day 6	Day 7
Week 1							
Week 2							
Week 3							
Week 4							
Week 5							

January 1: _____
_____
_____
_____

January 2: _____
_____
_____
_____

January 3: _____
_____
_____
_____

January 4: _____
_____
_____
_____

January 5: _____
_____
_____
_____

January 6: _____
_____
_____
_____

January ■ The Importance of Prayer

January 7: _____

_____

_____

January 8: _____

_____

_____

January 9: _____

_____

_____

January 10: _____

_____

_____

January 11: _____

_____

_____

January 12: _____

_____

_____

January 13: _____

_____

_____

January 14: _____

_____

_____

January 15: _____

_____

_____

January 16: _____

_____

_____

January 17: _____

_____

_____

January 18: _____

_____

_____

January 19:

January 20:

January 21:

January 22:

January 23:

January 24:

January 25:

January 26:

January 27:

January 28:

January 29:

January 30:

January 31: _____

_____

_____

_____

JANUARY — DAILY BIBLE READING

Date	Morning	Evening	✓	Date	Morning	Evening	✓
1	Matthew 1	Genesis 1, 2, 3		17	Matthew 12:1-23	Genesis 41, 42	
2	Matthew 2	Genesis 4, 5, 6		18	Matthew 12:24-50	Genesis 43, 44, 45	
3	Matthew 3	Genesis 7, 8, 9		19	Matthew 13:1-30	Genesis 46, 47, 48	
4	Matthew 4	Genesis 10, 11, 12		20	Matthew 13:31-58	Genesis 49, 50	
5	Matthew 5:1-26	Genesis 13, 14, 15		21	Matthew 14:1-21	Exodus 1, 2, 3	
6	Matthew 5:27-48	Genesis 16, 17		22	Matthew 14:22-36	Exodus 4, 5, 6	
7	Matthew 6:1-18	Genesis 18, 19		23	Matthew 15:1-20	Exodus 7, 8	
8	Matthew 6:19-34	Genesis 20, 21, 22		24	Matthew 15:21-39	Exodus 9, 10, 11	
9	Matthew 7	Genesis 23, 24		25	Matthew 16	Exodus 12, 13	
10	Matthew 8:1-17	Genesis 25, 26		26	Matthew 17	Exodus 14, 15	
11	Matthew 8:18-34	Genesis 27, 28		27	Matthew 18:1-20	Exodus 16, 17, 18	
12	Matthew 9:1-17	Genesis 29, 30		28	Matthew 18:21-35	Exodus 19, 20	
13	Matthew 9:18-38	Genesis 31, 32		29	Matthew 19	Exodus 21, 22	
14	Matthew 10:1-20	Genesis 33, 34, 35		30	Matthew 20:1-16	Exodus 23, 24	
15	Matthew 10:21-42	Genesis 36, 37, 38		31	Matthew 20:17-34	Exodus 25, 26	
16	Matthew 11	Genesis 39, 40					

NOTES:

_____

_____

_____

_____

_____

_____

_____

February
THE IMPORTANCE OF GOD'S WORD

 Scripture of the Month

"Thy word is a lamp unto my feet, and a light unto my path" (Psalm 119:105).

 Inspirational Thought

Meditating on God's Word helps to ignite and build your faith in Him.

 Prayer for the Month

Dear heavenly Father, I come to Your throne with joy unspeakable, as well as an open heart and mind for You to impart Your divine instructions found in the Holy Scriptures in me. Lord, help me to study Your Word, meditate on it, and hide it in my heart so that I might not sin against You. Lord, give me an appetite for Your Holy Scriptures and help me to rightly divide the Word of truth. Show me the importance of Your Word that I may know You better and in a real way as I read and study the Bible, which is my roadmap to eternity. Please, Lord, keep Your Holy Scriptures embedded in my mind that I may use Your Word in the time of need. Teach me how to become sharp as a two-edged sword in the Bible so that I can combat the attacks of Satan. All these many blessings I ask in the name of Your Son Jesus Christ. Amen!

 Monthly Challenge

For this month, memorize three (3) scriptures each week. Remember God's Word is combat material against the devil.

 Daily Checklist

Each day, answer the six questions. Once you have answered them, place a checkmark in the box on the Daily Checklist chart.

1. Did you pray today?
2. Did you read a scripture(s)?
3. Did you pray for someone? Who?
4. Did you fast today?
5. Did you witness to someone about Jesus?
6. What did you receive from the Lord today?

DAILY CHECKLIST	Day 1	Day 2	Day 3	Day 4	Day 5	Day 6	Day 7
Week 1							
Week 2							
Week 3							
Week 4							
Week 5							

February ■ The Importance of God's Word

February 1: _____
_____
_____
_____

February 2: _____
_____
_____
_____

February 3: _____
_____
_____
_____

February 4: _____
_____
_____
_____

February 5: _____
_____
_____
_____

February 6: _____
_____
_____
_____

Be BAD! Prayer Journal

February 7: _____

_____

_____

_____

February 8: _____

_____

_____

_____

February 9: _____

_____

_____

_____

February 10: _____

_____

_____

_____

February 11: _____

_____

_____

_____

February 12: _____

_____

_____

_____

February 13:

February 14:

February 15:

February 16:

February 17:

February 18:

February 19:

February 20:

February 21:

February 22:

February 23:

February 24:

February ■ The Importance of God's Word

February 25: _____

_____

_____

_____

February 26: _____

_____

_____

_____

February 27: _____

_____

_____

_____

February 28: _____

_____

_____

_____

February 29: _____

_____

_____

_____

Be BAD! Prayer Journal

FEBRUARY—DAILY BIBLE READING

Date	Morning	Evening	✓
1	Matthew 21:1-22	Exodus 27, 28	
2	Matthew 21:23-46	Exodus 29, 30	
3	Matthew 22:1-22	Exodus 31, 32, 33	
4	Matthew 22:23-46	Exodus 34, 35	
5	Matthew 23:1-22	Exodus 36, 37, 38	
6	Matthew 23:23-39	Exodus 39, 40	
7	Matthew 24:1-28	Leviticus 1, 2, 3	
8	Matthew 24:29-51	Leviticus 4, 5	
9	Matthew 25:1-30	Leviticus 6, 7	
10	Matthew 25:31-46	Leviticus 8, 9, 10	
11	Matthew 26:1-25	Leviticus 11, 12	
12	Matthew 26:26-50	Leviticus 13	
13	Matthew 26:51-75	Leviticus 14	
14	Matthew 27:1-26	Leviticus 15, 16	
15	Matthew 27:27-50	Leviticus 17, 18	
16	Matthew 27:51-66	Leviticus 19, 20	
17	Matthew 28	Leviticus 21, 22	
18	Mark 1:1-22	Leviticus 23, 24	
19	Mark 1:23-45	Leviticus 25	
20	Mark 2	Leviticus 26, 27	
21	Mark 3:1-19	Numbers 1, 2	
22	Mark 3:20-35	Numbers 3, 4	
23	Mark 4:1-20	Numbers 5, 6	
24	Mark 4:21-41	Numbers 7, 8	
25	Mark 5:1-20	Numbers 9, 10, 11	
26	Mark 5:21-43	Numbers 12, 13, 14	
27	Mark 6:1-29	Numbers 15, 16	
28*	Mark 6:30-56; 7:1-13	Numbers 17, 18, 19, 20	

*Years when there is a February 29th, split the reading between the 28th and 29th.

NOTES:

_____
_____
_____
_____
_____
_____
_____
_____
_____
_____
_____
_____

March
THE IMPORTANCE OF FASTING

 ### Scripture of the Month

"But thou, when thou fastest, anoint thine head, and wash thy face; That thou appear not unto men to fast, but unto thy Father which is in secret: and thy Father, which seeth in secret, shall reward thee openly" (Matthew 6:17-18).

 ### Inspirational Thought

Fasting coupled with prayer is the key to developing a close relationship with God. You can't go wrong when you pray daily and fast often with sincerity and purity.

 ### Prayer for the Month

Gracious and sovereign Savior, thank You for bringing me this far in this year. This month, I want to give of myself in a sacrificial way. Lord, reveal to me the importance of consecrating my life through fasting. As I give myself sacrificially, Lord, I need You to mold me and make me a vessel of honor that You can use. Lord, clean me up. Clean my mind – sanctify the atmosphere of my mind. Clean my heart. Create in me a clean heart and renew a right spirit within me. Clean my soul and spirit man that I may become an instrument for Your divine service. And, Lord, as I give myself in consecration to You, strengthen the inner man, pour into me Your magnificent power from above, and I will be careful to give You all the praise and honor. In Jesus' name, I pray. Amen!

 ### Monthly Challenge

Give yourself to fasting at least one (1) day a week in accordance with God's directions. Fasting as God instructs will build you up spiritually and help you weaken the flesh.

 ### Daily Checklist

Each day, answer the six questions. Once you have answered them, place a checkmark in the box on the Daily Checklist chart.

1. Did you pray today?
2. Did you read a scripture(s)?
3. Did you pray for someone? Who?
4. Did you fast today?
5. Did you witness to someone about Jesus?
6. What did you receive from the Lord today?

Be BAD! Prayer Journal

DAILY CHECKLIST	Day 1	Day 2	Day 3	Day 4	Day 5	Day 6	Day 7
Week 1							
Week 2							
Week 3							
Week 4							
Week 5							

March 1: _____

_____

_____

_____

March 2: _____

_____

_____

_____

March 3: _____

_____

_____

_____

March 4: _____

_____

_____

_____

March 5: _____

_____

_____

_____

March 6:

March 7:

March 8:

March 9:

March 10:

March 11:

March 12:

March 13:

March 14:

March 15:

March 16:

March 17:

March ■ The Importance of Fasting

March 18:

March 19:

March 20:

March 21:

March 22:

March 23:

March 24: _____

March 25: _____

March 26: _____

March 27: _____

March 28: _____

March 29: _____

March 30: _____

_____

_____

_____

March 31: _____

_____

_____

_____

MARCH—DAILY BIBLE READING

Date	Morning	Evening	✓	Date	Morning	Evening	✓
1	Mark 7:14-37	Numbers 21, 22, 23, 24		17	Mark 15:1-25	Deuteronomy 30, 31	
2	Mark 8:1-21	Numbers 25, 26, 27		18	Mark 15:26-47	Deuteronomy 32, 33, 34	
3	Mark 8:22-38	Numbers 28, 29, 30		19	Mark 16	Joshua 1, 2, 3	
4	Mark 9:1-29	Numbers 31, 32, 33		20	Luke 1:1-20	Joshua 4, 5, 6	
5	Mark 9:30-50	Numbers 34, 35, 36		21	Luke 1:21-38	Joshua 7, 8, 9	
6	Mark 10:1-31	Deuteronomy 1, 2		22	Luke 1:39-56	Joshua 10, 11, 12	
7	Mark 10:32-52	Deuteronomy 3, 4		23	Luke 1:57-80	Joshua 13, 14, 15	
8	Mark 11:1-18	Deuteronomy 5, 6, 7		24	Luke 2:1-24	Joshua 16, 17, 18	
9	Mark 11:19-33	Deuteronomy 8, 9, 10		25	Luke 2:25-52	Joshua 19, 20, 21	
10	Mark 12:1-27	Deuteronomy 11, 12, 13		26	Luke 3	Joshua 22, 23, 24	
11	Mark 12:28-44	Deuteronomy 14, 15, 16		27	Luke 4:1-30	Judges 1, 2, 3	
12	Mark 13:1-20	Deuteronomy 17, 18, 19		28	Luke 4:31-44	Judges 4, 5, 6	
13	Mark 13:21-37	Deuteronomy 20, 21, 22		29	Luke 5:1-16	Judges 7, 8	
14	Mark 14:1-26	Deuteronomy 23, 24, 25		30	Luke 5:17-39	Judges 9, 10	
15	Mark 14:27-53	Deuteronomy 26, 27		31	Luke 6:1-26	Judges 11, 12	
16	Mark 14:54-72	Deuteronomy 28, 29					

NOTES:

_____

_____

_____

April
HAVE FAITH IN GOD

 ### Scripture of the Month

"So faith cometh by hearing, and hearing by the word of God" (Romans 10:17).

 ### Inspirational Thought

Faith put into action will change reality (what is) into what it is destined to be according to the divine will of God.

 ### Prayer for the Month

Lord Jesus, You told me in Your Word that without faith it is impossible to please You (Hebrews 11:6). Lord, I want to please You in all that I say and do. I pray now that You will help me to stay focused on You, trusting You in every area of my life. Lord, destroy any doubt within my mind and heart. Implant that mustard seed faith in me so that I will move mountains and make the impossibilities of my life possible through You. Lord, You also let me know in Your Holy Scriptures that faith comes by hearing and hearing by the Word of God (Romans 10:17). Help me to continually feed my mind and heart with Your Word so that my faith in You will remain strong. Lord, I will trust You with everything that is within me, and I will diligently seek You by faith. Manifest Your power within me as I walk this walk of faith. I thank You in advance for answered prayers. In Jesus' name. Amen!

 ### Monthly Challenge

Whatever problem arises, put your *total trust* in God. Do not attempt to handle anything on your own. Trust in the Lord with all your heart and do not lean on your own understanding. Acknowledge God in everything. He will provide the guidance and answers you need.

 ### Daily Checklist

Each day, answer the six questions. Once you have answered them, place a checkmark in the box on the Daily Checklist chart.

1. Did you pray today?
2. Did you read a scripture(s)?
3. Did you pray for someone? Who?
4. Did you fast today?
5. Did you witness to someone about Jesus?
6. What did you receive from the Lord today?

April ■ Have Faith in God

DAILY CHECKLIST	Day 1	Day 2	Day 3	Day 4	Day 5	Day 6	Day 7
Week 1							
Week 2							
Week 3							
Week 4							
Week 5							

April 1: _____

_____

_____

April 2: _____

_____

_____

April 3: _____

_____

_____

April 4: _____

_____

_____

April 5: _____

_____

_____

April 6: _____

_____

_____

April 7: _____

_____

_____

April 8: _____

_____

_____

April 9: _____

_____

_____

April 10: _____

_____

_____

April 11: _____

_____

_____

April 12:

April 13:

April 14:

April 15:

April 16:

April 17:

April 18: _____

_____

_____

_____

April 19: _____

_____

_____

_____

April 20: _____

_____

_____

_____

April 21: _____

_____

_____

_____

April 22: _____

_____

_____

_____

April 23: _____

_____

_____

_____

April ■ Have Faith in God

April 24: _____

April 25: _____

April 26: _____

April 27: _____

April 28: _____

April 29: _____

Be BAD! Prayer Journal

April 30: _____

_____

_____

_____

APRIL—DAILY BIBLE READING

Date	Morning	Evening	✓
1	Luke 6:27-49	Judges 13, 14, 15	
2	Luke 7:1-30	Judges 16, 17, 18	
3	Luke 7:31-50	Judges 19, 20, 21	
4	Luke 8:1-25	Ruth 1, 2, 3, 4	
5	Luke 8:26-56	1 Samuel 1, 2, 3	
6	Luke 9:1-17	1 Samuel 4, 5, 6	
7	Luke 9:18-36	1 Samuel 7, 8, 9	
8	Luke 9:37-62	1 Samuel 10, 11, 12	
9	Luke 10:1-24	1 Samuel 13, 14	
10	Luke 10:25-42	1 Samuel 15, 16	
11	Luke 11:1-28	1 Samuel 17, 18	
12	Luke 11:29-54	1 Samuel 19, 20, 21	
13	Luke 12:1-31	1 Samuel 22, 23, 24	
14	Luke 12:32-59	1 Samuel 25, 26	
15	Luke 13:1-22	1 Samuel 27, 28, 29	
16	Luke 13:23-35	1 Samuel 30, 31	
17	Luke 14:1-24	2 Samuel 1, 2	
18	Luke 14:25-35	2 Samuel 3, 4, 5	
19	Luke 15:1-10	2 Samuel 6, 7, 8	
20	Luke 15:11-32	2 Samuel 9, 10, 11	
21	Luke 16	2 Samuel 12, 13	
22	Luke 17:1-19	2 Samuel 14, 15	
23	Luke 17:20-37	2 Samuel 16, 17, 18	
24	Luke 18:1-23	2 Samuel 19, 20	
25	Luke 18:24-43	2 Samuel 21, 22	
26	Luke 19:1-27	2 Samuel 23, 24	
27	Luke 19:28-48	1 Kings 1, 2	
28	Luke 20:1-26	1 Kings 3, 4, 5	
29	Luke 20:27-47	1 Kings 6, 7	
30	Luke 21:1-29	1 Kings 8, 9	

NOTES:

_____

_____

_____

_____

_____

_____

_____

_____

May
FULFILLING THE PURPOSE OF GOD

 Scripture of the Month

"For I know the thoughts that I think toward you, saith the Lord, thoughts of peace, and not of evil, to give you an expected end" (Jeremiah 29:11).

 Inspirational Thought

Through prayer, you can maintain a spirit of obedience and a willingness to sacrifice, which are essential tools for fulfilling the purpose of God.

 Prayer for the Month

Dear Jesus, I am very grateful to You for life. Lord, lead and guide me as I take this journey to eternity. Please show me Your purpose for my existence and then teach me how to walk on the path You have designed for me. Help me to realize that without purpose, I'm simply existing. Teach me how to live a purposeful life in You because without You I am nothing, but with You I'm destined for greatness. Please, Lord, keep me motivated to go to the level You desire me to go both spiritually and naturally. No matter what the task, Lord, I can do all things through You who strengthens me. Bless my talents and gifts that they may blossom and be used for the building of Your kingdom and in preparation for Your return. Thank You that I have a life of purpose designed by You, the master designer. I anticipate a harvest of blessings as I walk this purposed-filled life in You. I praise You now for my life. Thank You for choosing me to live for You. Amen!

 Monthly Challenge

Write down your purpose in God. Write down a goal you desire to accomplish each week that will help you fulfill your God-ordained purpose. Remember you were created for a purpose. It is up to you to work toward fulfilling your purpose in God.

 Daily Checklist

Each day, answer the six questions. Once you have answered them, place a checkmark in the box on the Daily Checklist chart.

1. Did you pray today?
2. Did you read a scripture(s)?
3. Did you pray for someone? Who?
4. Did you fast today?
5. Did you witness to someone about Jesus?
6. What did you receive from the Lord today?

DAILY CHECKLIST	Day 1	Day 2	Day 3	Day 4	Day 5	Day 6	Day 7
Week 1							
Week 2							
Week 3							
Week 4							
Week 5							

May 1: _____

May 2: _____

May 3: _____

May 4: _____

May 5: _____

May ■ Fulfilling the Purpose of God

May 6: _____

_____

_____

_____

May 7: _____

_____

_____

_____

May 8: _____

_____

_____

_____

May 9: _____

_____

_____

_____

May 10: _____

_____

_____

_____

May 11: _____

_____

_____

_____

May 12: _____

May 13: _____

May 14: _____

May 15: _____

May 16: _____

May 17: _____

May ■ Fulfilling the Purpose of God

May 18: _____

May 19: _____

May 20: _____

May 21: _____

May 22: _____

May 23: _____

May 24: _____

_____

_____

May 25: _____

_____

_____

May 26: _____

_____

_____

May 27: _____

_____

_____

May 28: _____

_____

_____

May 29: _____

_____

_____

May 30: _____

_____

_____

_____

May 31: _____

_____

_____

_____

MAY—DAILY BIBLE READING

Date	Morning	Evening	✓
1	Luke 21:20-38	1 Kings 10, 11	
2	Luke 22:1-20	1 Kings 12, 13	
3	Luke 22:21-46	1 Kings 14, 15	
4	Luke 22:47-71	1 Kings 16, 17, 18	
5	Luke 23:1-25	1 Kings 19, 20	
6	Luke 23:26-56	1 Kings 21, 22	
7	Luke 24:1-35	2 Kings 1, 2, 3	
8	Luke 24:36-53	2 Kings 4, 5, 6	
9	St. John 1:1-28	2 Kings 7, 8, 9	
10	St. John 1:29-51	2 Kings 10, 11, 12	
11	St. John 2	2 Kings 13, 14	
12	St. John 3:1-18	2 Kings 15, 16	
13	St. John 3:19-38	2 Kings 17, 18	
14	St. John 4:1-30	2 Kings 19, 20, 21	
15	St. John 4:31-54	2 Kings 22, 23	
16	St. John 5:1-24	2 Kings 24, 25	
17	St. John 5:25-47	1 Chronicles 1, 2, 3	
18	St. John 6:1-21	1 Chronicles 4, 5, 6	
19	St. John 6:22-44	1 Chronicles 7, 8, 9	
20	St. John 6:45-71	1 Chronicles 10, 11, 12	
21	St. John 7:1-27	1 Chronicles 13, 14, 15	
22	St. John 7:28-53	1 Chronicles 16, 17, 18	
23	St. John 8:1-27	1 Chronicles 19, 20, 21	
24	St. John 8:28-59	1 Chronicles 22, 23, 24	
25	St. John 9:1-23	1 Chronicles 25, 26, 27	
26	St. John 9:24-41	1 Chronicles 28, 29	
27	St. John 10:1-23	2 Chronicles 1, 2, 3	
28	St. John 10:24-42	2 Chronicles 4, 5, 6	
29	St. John 11:1-29	2 Chronicles 7, 8, 9	
30	St. John 11:30-57	2 Chronicles 10, 11, 12	
31	St. John 12:1-26	2 Chronicles 13, 14	

NOTES:

_____

_____

_____

June

BLESSED FOR SERVICE

 ### Scripture of the Month

"Blessed are they which do hunger and thirst after righteousness: for they shall be filled" (Matthew 5:6).

 ### Inspirational Thought

Being blessed characterizes your relationship with God. Chase after God through prayer.

 ### Prayer for the Month

Lord, send Your Holy Spirit now and minister to me. Reveal to me the divine assignments You desire me to perform. Give me what to do and show me how to do it. Let me be blessed as I follow Your instructions. Give me a keen spiritual ear to hear what You are saying. Remove all dullness from my hearing and let me hear Your directions clearly. Let me move forward in You, rendering service for Your honor and glory. Let me be blessed beyond measure as I serve You. In Jesus' name, I pray. Amen!

 ### Monthly Challenge

Each week, give one (1) day of service to your church. Only what you do for Christ will count in the end.

 ### Daily Checklist

Each day, answer the six questions. Once you have answered them, place a checkmark in the box on the Daily Checklist chart.

1. Did you pray today?
2. Did you read a scripture(s)?
3. Did you pray for someone? Who?
4. Did you fast today?
5. Did you witness to someone about Jesus?
6. What did you receive from the Lord today?

DAILY CHECKLIST	Day 1	Day 2	Day 3	Day 4	Day 5	Day 6	Day 7
Week 1							
Week 2							
Week 3							
Week 4							
Week 5							

June 1: _____

_____
_____

June 2: _____

_____
_____

June 3: _____

_____
_____

June 4: _____

_____
_____

June 5: _____

_____
_____

June 6: _____

_____
_____

Be BAD! Prayer Journal

June 7: _____
_____
_____
_____

June 8: _____
_____
_____
_____

June 9: _____
_____
_____
_____

June 10: _____
_____
_____
_____

June 11: _____
_____
_____
_____

June 12: _____
_____
_____
_____

June ■ Blessed for Service

June 13: _____

_____

_____

June 14: _____

_____

_____

June 15: _____

_____

_____

June 16: _____

_____

_____

June 17: _____

_____

_____

June 18: _____

_____

_____

June 19: _____

_____

_____

June 20: _____

_____

_____

June 21: _____

_____

_____

June 22: _____

_____

_____

June 23: _____

_____

_____

June 24: _____

_____

_____

June ■ Blessed for Service

June 25: _____

June 26: _____

June 27: _____

June 28: _____

June 29: _____

June 30: _____

JUNE—DAILY BIBLE READING

Date	Morning	Evening	✓
1	St. John 12:27-50	2 Chronicles 15, 16	
2	St. John 13:1-20	2 Chronicles 17, 18	
3	St. John 13:21-38	2 Chronicles 19, 20	
4	St. John 14	2 Chronicles 21, 22	
5	St. John 15	2 Chronicles 23, 24	
6	St. John 16	2 Chronicles 25, 26, 27	
7	St. John 17	2 Chronicles 28, 29	
8	St. John 18:1-18	2 Chronicles 30, 31	
9	St. John 18:19-40	2 Chronicles 32, 33	
10	St. John 19:1-22	2 Chronicles 34, 35, 36	
11	St. John 19:23-42	Ezra 1, 2	
12	St. John 20	Ezra 3, 4, 5	
13	St. John 21	Ezra 6, 7, 8	
14	Acts 1	Ezra 9, 10	
15	Acts 2:1-21	Nehemiah 1, 2, 3	
16	Acts 2:22-47	Nehemiah 4, 5, 6	
17	Acts 3	Nehemiah 7, 8, 9	
18	Acts 4:1-22	Nehemiah 10, 11	
19	Acts 4:23-37	Nehemiah 12, 13	
20	Acts 5:1-21	Esther 1, 2	
21	Acts 5:22-42	Esther 3, 4, 5	
22	Acts 6	Esther 6, 7, 8	
23	Acts 7:1-21	Esther 9, 10	
24	Acts 7:22-43	Job 1, 2	
25	Acts 7:44-60	Job 3, 4	
26	Acts 8:1-25	Job 5, 6, 7	
27	Acts 8:26-40	Job 8, 9, 10	
28	Acts 9:1-21	Job 11, 12, 13	
29	Acts 9:22-43	Job 14, 15, 16	
30	Acts 10:1-23	Job 17, 18, 19	

NOTES:

July
APPOINTED TO BE ANOINTED

 ### Scripture of the Month

The Spirit of the Lord God is upon me; because the Lord hath anointed me to preach good tidings unto the meek; he hath sent me to bind up the brokenhearted, to proclaim liberty to the captives, and the opening of the prison to them that are bound; to proclaim the acceptable year of the Lord, and the day of vengeance of our God, to comfort all that mourn; to appoint unto them that mourn in Zion, to give unto them beauty for ashes, the oil of joy for mourning, the garment of praise for the spirit of heaviness; that they might be called trees of righteousness, the planting of the Lord, that He might be glorified. (Isaiah 61:1-3)

 ### Inspirational Thought

God's anointing empowers you to handle any situation. God appointed you for Himself so you can give Him your mind, body, soul, and spirit completely in prayer.

 ### Prayer for the Month

Gracious and heavenly Father, thank You for appointing and anointing me to do battle for Your kingdom. Give me insight continually on the importance of prayer and fasting in order to receive Your power within. Right now, breathe the breath of Your anointing, and let it engulf me from the crown of my head to the soles of my feet. Lord, empower me with Your authority, courage, wisdom, and strength. Allow me to experience spiritual growth and a powerful awakening of Your anointing as I give myself totally to You. I ask all of this in the name of Your Son, Jesus. Amen!

 ### Monthly Challenge

Witness to at least one (1) person each day, providing the good news of Jesus Christ. Jesus Christ is the answer for the world today.

 ### Daily Checklist

Each day, answer the six questions. Once you have answered them, place a checkmark in the box on the Daily Checklist chart.

1. Did you pray today?
2. Did you read a scripture(s)?
3. Did you pray for someone? Who?
4. Did you fast today?
5. Did you witness to someone about Jesus?
6. What did you receive from the Lord today?

Be BAD! Prayer Journal

DAILY CHECKLIST	Day 1	Day 2	Day 3	Day 4	Day 5	Day 6	Day 7
Week 1							
Week 2							
Week 3							
Week 4							
Week 5							

July 1: _____

_____

_____

_____

July 2: _____

_____

_____

_____

July 3: _____

_____

_____

_____

July 4: _____

_____

_____

_____

July 5: _____

_____

_____

_____

July ■ Appointed to be Anointed

July 6: _____

July 7: _____

July 8: _____

July 9: _____

July 10: _____

July 11: _____

July 12: _____

_____

_____

July 13: _____

_____

_____

July 14: _____

_____

_____

July 15: _____

_____

_____

July 16: _____

_____

_____

July 17: _____

_____

_____

July 18:

July 19:

July 20:

July 21:

July 22:

July 23:

July 24: _____

_____

_____

July 25: _____

_____

_____

July 26: _____

_____

_____

July 27: _____

_____

_____

July 28: _____

_____

_____

July 29: _____

_____

_____

July 30: _____

July 31: _____

JULY—DAILY BIBLE READING

Date	Morning	Evening	✓	Date	Morning	Evening	✓
1	Acts 10:24-48	Job 20, 21		17	Acts 20:17-38	Psalm 18, 19	
2	Acts 11	Job 22, 23, 24		18	Acts 21:1-17	Psalm 20, 21, 22	
3	Acts 12	Job 25, 26, 27		19	Acts 21:18-40	Psalm 23, 24, 25	
4	Acts 13:1-25	Job 28, 29		20	Acts 22	Psalm 26, 27, 28	
5	Acts 13:26-52	Job 30, 31		21	Acts 23:1-15	Psalm 29, 30	
6	Acts 14	Job 32, 33		22	Acts 23:16-35	Psalm 31, 32	
7	Acts 15:1-21	Job 34, 35		23	Acts 24	Psalm 33, 34	
8	Acts 15:22-41	Job 36, 37		24	Acts 25	Psalm 35, 36	
9	Acts 16:1-21	Job 38, 39, 40		25	Acts 26	Psalm 37, 38, 39	
10	Acts 16:22-40	Job 41, 42		26	Acts 27:1-26	Psalm 40, 41, 42	
11	Acts 17:1-15	Psalm 1, 2, 3		27	Acts 27:27-44	Psalm 43, 44, 45	
12	Acts 17:16-34	Psalm 4, 5, 6		28	Acts 28	Psalm 46, 47, 48	
13	Acts 18	Psalm 7, 8, 9		29	Romans 1	Psalm 49, 50	
14	Acts 19:1-20	Psalm 10, 11, 12		30	Romans 2	Psalm 51, 52, 53	
15	Acts 19:21-41	Psalm 13, 14, 15		31	Romans 3	Psalm 54, 55, 56	
16	Acts 20:1-16	Psalm 16, 17					

NOTES:

August
WALK IN YOUR DELIVERANCE

 Scripture of the Month

"This I say then, Walk in the Spirit, and ye shall not fulfill the lust of the flesh" (Galatians 5:16).

 Inspirational Thought

Maintaining your walk of deliverance keeps you free from the devil's attempts to interfere.

 Prayer for the Month

Gracious Father, the one who knows all things and can perform anything, help me to immediately recognize the need for deliverance when I struggle because of bondage and strongholds. Send Your spiritual power of deliverance now. Teach me how to walk in my deliverance by constantly communicating with You. Don't let me be tricked by Satan. Lord, let me realize that every obstacle can present an opportunity to improve my condition when I stand firm on Your promises outlined in Your Word. God, give me the security to know You will always be there for me, and You will never leave or forsake me. Overshadow me now with the power of Your love and peace. Let Your Holy Spirit minister to me, instructing and directing me to a life of continuous freedom. All these blessings I ask in the name of Your precious Son, Jesus. Amen.

 Monthly Challenge

Write down any struggles or obstacles Satan tries to bring to you. Declare to Satan: "I will not be defeated. I am delivered by the power of Jesus' blood."

 Daily Checklist

Each day, answer the six questions. Once you have answered them, place a checkmark in the box on the Daily Checklist chart.

1. Did you pray today?
2. Did you read a scripture(s)?
3. Did you pray for someone? Who?
4. Did you fast today?
5. Did you witness to someone about Jesus?
6. What did you receive from the Lord today?

DAILY CHECKLIST	Day 1	Day 2	Day 3	Day 4	Day 5	Day 6	Day 7
Week 1							
Week 2							
Week 3							
Week 4							
Week 5							

August ■ Walk in your Deliverance

August 1: _____

_____

_____

August 2: _____

_____

_____

August 3: _____

_____

_____

August 4: _____

_____

_____

August 5: _____

_____

_____

August 6: _____

_____

_____

August 7: _____

August 8: _____

August 9: _____

August 10: _____

August 11: _____

August 12: _____

August 13: _____

_____

_____

August 14: _____

_____

_____

August 15: _____

_____

_____

August 16: _____

_____

_____

August 17: _____

_____

_____

August 18: _____

_____

_____

Be BAD! Prayer Journal

August 19: _____

_____

_____

_____

August 20: _____

_____

_____

_____

August 21: _____

_____

_____

_____

August 22: _____

_____

_____

_____

August 23: _____

_____

_____

_____

August 24: _____

_____

_____

_____

August 25:

August 26:

August 27:

August 28:

August 29:

August 30:

Be BAD! Prayer Journal

August 31: _____

_____
_____
_____

AUGUST—DAILY BIBLE READING

Date	Morning	Evening	✓	Date	Morning	Evening	✓
1	Romans 4	Psalm 57, 58, 59		17	Romans 16	Psalm 97, 98, 99	
2	Romans 5	Psalm 60, 61, 62		18	1 Corinthians 1	Psalm 100,101,102	
3	Romans 6	Psalm 63, 64, 65		19	1 Corinthians 2	Psalm 103,104	
4	Romans 7	Psalm 66, 67		20	1 Corinthians 3	Psalm 105,106	
5	Romans 8:1-21	Psalm 68, 69		21	1 Corinthians 4	Psalm 107,108,109	
6	Romans 8:22-39	Psalm 70, 71		22	1 Corinthians 5	Psalm 110,111,112	
7	Romans 9:1-15	Psalm 72, 73		23	1 Corinthians 6	Psalm 113,114,115	
8	Romans 9:16-33	Psalm 74, 75, 76		24	1 Corinthians 7:1-19	Psalm 116,117,118	
9	Romans 10	Psalm 77, 78		25	1 Corinthians 7:20-40	Psalm 119:1-88	
10	Romans 11:1-18	Psalm 79, 80		26	1 Corinthians 8	Psalm 119:89-176	
11	Romans 11:19-36	Psalm 81, 82, 83		27	1 Corinthians 9	Psalm 120,121,122	
12	Romans 12	Psalm 84, 85, 86		28	1 Corinthians 10:1-18	Psalm 123,124,125	
13	Romans 13	Psalm 87, 88		29	1 Corinthians10:19-33	Psalm 126,127,128	
14	Romans 14	Psalm 89, 90		30	1 Corinthians11:1-16	Psalm 129,130,131	
15	Romans 15:1-13	Psalm 91, 92, 93		31	1 Corinthians11:17-34	Psalm 132,133,134	
16	Romans 15:14-33	Psalm 94, 95, 96					

NOTES:

_____
_____
_____
_____
_____
_____
_____

September
LIVING A VICTORIOUS LIFE IN GOD

 ### Scripture of the Month

"Behold, I give unto you power to tread on serpents and scorpions, and over all the power of the enemy; and nothing shall by any means hurt you" (Luke 10:19).

 ### Inspirational Thought

There will always be a "better" in your circumstances, so don't worry about adversity; you already have the victory.

 ### Prayer for the Month

Heavenly Father, thank You for life and the air that I breathe. Lord, at times I feel I might let You down because of the adversity that comes my way. Lord, I cry out to You now. Give me spiritual eyes to see and spiritual ears to hear that because of who You are, I have the victory. The devil is already defeated. God, I long to please You in all I do. I know that as long as I have You as the director of my life, I will constantly live victoriously. Lord, impart to me daily that I am not the victim but the victor, and I will be victorious in You. Teach me how to let go of the past that I might take hold of my future. Lord, I believe the adverse things that occur in my life are just tiny matters compared to Your power that lives in me. I thank You now for the victory. I bless Your name. I praise Your name. I adore You, and I will live a victorious life. In Jesus' name. Amen!

 ### Monthly Challenge

Affirm and repeat the following statements daily: "I will not fail in my efforts. I will succeed and be victorious in God." You make the choice to live a blessed life.

 ### Daily Checklist

Each day, answer the six questions. Once you have answered them, place a checkmark in the box on the Daily Checklist chart.

1. Did you pray today?
2. Did you read a scripture(s)?
3. Did you pray for someone? Who?
4. Did you fast today?
5. Did you witness to someone about Jesus?
6. What did you receive from the Lord today?

DAILY CHECKLIST	Day 1	Day 2	Day 3	Day 4	Day 5	Day 6	Day 7
Week 1							
Week 2							
Week 3							
Week 4							
Week 5							

September 1: _____

_____

_____

September 2: _____

_____

_____

September 3: _____

_____

_____

September 4: _____

_____

_____

September 5: _____

_____

_____

September ■ Living a Victorious Life in God

September 6:

September 7:

September 8:

September 9:

September 10:

September 11:

Be BAD! Prayer Journal

September 12:

September 13:

September 14:

September 15:

September 16:

September 17:

September 18: _____

_____
_____
_____

September 19: _____

_____
_____
_____

September 20: _____

_____
_____
_____

September 21: _____

_____
_____
_____

September 22: _____

_____
_____
_____

September 23: _____

_____
_____
_____

September 24:

September 25:

September 26:

September 27:

September 28:

September 29:

September 30: _____

_____

_____

_____

SEPTEMBER—DAILY BIBLE READING

Date	Morning	Evening	✓
1	1 Corinthians 12	Psalm 135, 136	
2	1 Corinthians 13	Psalm 137, 138, 139	
3	1 Corinthians 14:1-20	Psalm 140, 141, 142	
4	1 Corinthians 14:21-40	Psalm 143, 144, 145	
5	1 Corinthians 15:1-28	Psalm 146, 147	
6	1 Corinthians 15:29-58	Psalm 148, 149, 150	
7	1 Corinthians 16	Proverbs 1, 2	
8	2 Corinthians 1	Proverbs 3, 4, 5	
9	2 Corinthians 2	Proverbs 6, 7	
10	2 Corinthians 3	Proverbs 8, 9	
11	2 Corinthians 4	Proverbs 10, 11, 12	
12	2 Corinthians 5	Proverbs 13, 14, 15	
13	2 Corinthians 6	Proverbs 16, 17, 18	
14	2 Corinthians 7	Proverbs 19, 20, 21	
15	2 Corinthians 8	Proverbs 22, 23, 24	
16	2 Corinthians 9	Proverbs 25, 26	
17	2 Corinthians 10	Proverbs 27, 28, 29	
18	2 Corinthians 11:1-15	Proverbs 30, 31	
19	2 Corinthians 11:16-33	Ecclesiastes 1, 2, 3	
20	2 Corinthians 12	Ecclesiastes 4, 5, 6	
21	2 Corinthians 13	Ecclesiastes 7, 8, 9	
22	Galatians 1	Ecclesiastes 10, 11, 12	
23	Galatians 2	Song of Solomon 1, 2, 3	
24	Galatians 3	Song of Solomon 4, 5	
25	Galatians 4	Song of Solomon 6, 7, 8	
26	Galatians 5	Isaiah 1, 2	
27	Galatians 6	Isaiah 3, 4	
28	Ephesians 1	Isaiah 5, 6	
29	Ephesians 2	Isaiah 7, 8	
30	Ephesians 3	Isaiah 9, 10	

NOTES:

_____

_____

_____

_____

_____

_____

October

GOD'S FAVOR

 Scripture of the Month

"For thou, Lord, wilt bless the righteous; with favor wilt thou compass him as with a shield" (Psalm 5:12).

 Inspirational Thought

God's favor is a blessing and a privilege. God's favor means having fantastic approval validated by an omnipotent resource.

 Prayer for the Month

Master, the self-existent one, I thank You for bestowing all of Your richest favors on me. I thank You because You daily load me with benefits that keep me sustained. Lord Jesus, I value Your awesome presence. Please continue to show me Your favor every second, minute, and hour of the day. I praise You, Lord, because even when I feel like everything is falling apart, You show up and remind me You are always with me. I don't have to worry because You have it all under control. Thank You, Lord, for the overflow of Your Fantastic Approval Validated by an Omnipotent Resource – You! Lord, because of Your favor I have the Faith, Assurance, Victory, and Opportunity to Receive all You have for me. Thank You, God, for favoring me. Amen!

 Monthly Challenge

Perform a special act of kindness for one person each week. When you give, God will give back to you in greater measure than what you gave.

 Daily Checklist

Each day, answer the six questions. Once you have answered them, place a checkmark in the box on the Daily Checklist chart.

1. Did you pray today?
2. Did you read a scripture(s)?
3. Did you pray for someone? Who?
4. Did you fast today?
5. Did you witness to someone about Jesus?
6. What did you receive from the Lord today?

October ■ God's Favor

DAILY CHECKLIST	Day 1	Day 2	Day 3	Day 4	Day 5	Day 6	Day 7
Week 1							
Week 2							
Week 3							
Week 4							
Week 5							

October 1: _____

_____

_____

_____

October 2: _____

_____

_____

_____

October 3: _____

_____

_____

_____

October 4: _____

_____

_____

_____

October 5: _____

_____

_____

_____

Be BAD! Prayer Journal

October 6: _____

October 7: _____

October 8: _____

October 9: _____

October 10: _____

October 11: _____

October 12:

October 13:

October 14:

October 15:

October 16:

October 17:

October 18: _____

October 19: _____

October 20: _____

October 21: _____

October 22: _____

October 23: _____

October ■ God's Favor

October 24: _____

October 25: _____

October 26: _____

October 27: _____

October 28: _____

October 29: _____

Be BAD! Prayer Journal

October 30: _____

_____

_____

_____

October 31: _____

_____

_____

_____

OCTOBER—DAILY BIBLE READING

Date	Morning	Evening	✓
1	Ephesians 4	Isaiah 11, 12, 13	
2	Ephesians 5:1-16	Isaiah 14, 15, 16	
3	Ephesians 5:17-33	Isaiah 17, 18, 19	
4	Ephesians 6	Isaiah 20, 21, 22	
5	Philippians 1	Isaiah 23, 24, 25	
6	Philippians 2	Isaiah 26, 27	
7	Philippians 3	Isaiah 28, 29	
8	Philippians 4	Isaiah 30, 31	
9	Colossians 1	Isaiah 32, 33	
10	Colossians 2	Isaiah 34, 35, 36	
11	Colossians 3	Isaiah 37, 38	
12	Colossians 4	Isaiah 39, 40	
13	1 Thessalonians 1	Isaiah 41, 42	
14	1 Thessalonians 2	Isaiah 43, 44	
15	1 Thessalonians 3	Isaiah 45, 46	
16	1 Thessalonians 4	Isaiah 47, 48, 49	

Date	Morning	Evening	✓
17	1 Thessalonians 5	Isaiah 50, 51, 52	
18	2 Thessalonians 1	Isaiah 53, 54, 55	
19	2 Thessalonians 2	Isaiah 56, 57, 58	
20	2 Thessalonians 3	Isaiah 59, 60, 61	
21	1 Timothy 1	Isaiah 62, 63, 64	
22	1 Timothy 2	Isaiah 65, 66	
23	1 Timothy 3	Jeremiah 1, 2	
24	1 Timothy 4	Jeremiah 3, 4, 5	
25	1 Timothy 5	Jeremiah 6, 7, 8	
26	1 Timothy 6	Jeremiah 9, 10, 11	
27	2 Timothy 1	Jeremiah 12, 13, 14	
28	2 Timothy 2	Jeremiah 15, 16, 17	
29	2 Timothy 3	Jeremiah 18, 19	
30	2 Timothy 4	Jeremiah 20, 21	
31	Titus 1	Jeremiah 22, 23	

NOTES:

_____

_____

_____

_____

November
GOD'S DIVINE WILL

 ### Scripture of the Month

"Teach me to do thy will; for thou art my God; thy spirit is good; lead me into the land of uprightness" (Psalm 143:10).

 ### Inspirational Thought

When you delight to do the will of God, His desire becomes your desire, which helps you to be comfortable in your walk with Him. Additionally, it seals the assurance within you that the end result of any situation will be for your good.

 ### Prayer for the Month

Dear Lord, my desire is to be in Your divine will. Lord, I ask You to crucify the flesh and don't let any flesh glory in Thy sight. Keep me in the center of your divine will. I know the thoughts You think toward me; they are good thoughts and not evil. Your divine will and plan for me will always be favorable because You will not allow anything meaningless to happen in my life. Lord, keep me covered with Your divine blood and power. I understand You know what is best for me, and I will trust You to move on my behalf in all situations. Lord, I thank You for being the God of promise and performance. You and only You can change a seemingly defeated circumstance into the reality of Your divine will just by the power of the words You speak. Lord, continue to order my steps for the path You have designed me to walk. I love You, Lord, with all my heart. All these blessings I ask in the name of Your Son, Jesus. Amen!

 ### Monthly Challenge

Ask God to teach you how to submit to His divine will daily. Journal all the instructions given by God and then obey Him. When you are willing and obedient, you will receive God's abundant supply of blessings.

 ### Daily Checklist

Each day, answer the six questions. Once you have answered them, place a checkmark in the box on the Daily Checklist chart.

1. Did you pray today?
2. Did you read a scripture(s)?
3. Did you pray for someone? Who?
4. Did you fast today?
5. Did you witness to someone about Jesus?
6. What did you receive from the Lord today?

Be BAD! Prayer Journal

DAILY CHECKLIST	Day 1	Day 2	Day 3	Day 4	Day 5	Day 6	Day 7
Week 1							
Week 2							
Week 3							
Week 4							
Week 5							

November 1: _____

_____

_____

_____

November 2: _____

_____

_____

_____

November 3: _____

_____

_____

_____

November 4: _____

_____

_____

_____

November 5: _____

_____

_____

_____

November ■ God's Divine Will

November 6:

November 7:

November 8:

November 9:

November 10:

November 11:

November 12:

November 13:

November 14:

November 15:

November 16:

November 17:

November 18:

November 19:

November 20:

November 21:

November 22:

November 23:

November 24:

November 25:

November 26:

November 27:

November 28:

November 29:

November 30:

NOVEMBER—DAILY BIBLE READING

Date	Morning	Evening	✓
1	Titus 2	Jeremiah 24, 25, 26	
2	Titus 3	Jeremiah 27, 28, 29	
3	Philemon 1	Jeremiah 30, 31	
4	Hebrews 1	Jeremiah 32, 33	
5	Hebrews 2	Jeremiah 34, 35, 36	
6	Hebrews 3	Jeremiah 37, 38, 39	
7	Hebrews 4	Jeremiah 40, 41, 42	
8	Hebrews 5	Jeremiah 43, 44, 45	
9	Hebrews 6	Jeremiah 46, 47	
10	Hebrews 7	Jeremiah 48, 49	
11	Hebrews 8	Jeremiah 50	
12	Hebrews 9	Jeremiah 51, 52	
13	Hebrews 10:1-18	Lamentations 1, 2	
14	Hebrews 10:19-39	Lamentations 3, 4, 5	
15	Hebrews 11:1-19	Ezekiel 1, 2	
16	Hebrews 11:20-40	Ezekiel 3, 4	
17	Hebrews 12	Ezekiel 5, 6, 7	
18	Hebrews 13	Ezekiel 8, 9, 10	
19	James 1	Ezekiel 11, 12, 13	
20	James 2	Ezekiel 14, 15	
21	James 3	Ezekiel 16, 17	
22	James 4	Ezekiel 18, 19	
23	James 5	Ezekiel 20, 21	
24	1 Peter 1	Ezekiel 22, 23	
25	1 Peter 2	Ezekiel 24, 25, 26	
26	1 Peter 3	Ezekiel 27, 28, 29	
27	1 Peter 4	Ezekiel 30, 31, 32	
28	1 Peter 5	Ezekiel 33, 34	
29	2 Peter 1	Ezekiel 35, 36	
30	2 Peter 2	Ezekiel 37, 38, 39	

NOTES:

December

GOD'S GIFT OF LOVE

 ### Scripture of the Month

"But God commendeth his love toward us, in that, while we were yet sinners, Christ died for us" (Romans 5:8).

 ### Inspirational Thought

The gift of God's love is priceless. God's love looks beyond all your faults, flaws, and failures. It sees a valuable vessel He can use in His kingdom.

 ### Prayer for the Month

Dear heavenly Father, thank You for sending Your priceless love gift, Jesus Christ, who shed His blood on the cross and died to cover my sins. That's love! No one in this world can ever provide the kind of love You give. Lord, I need Your love always abiding in me and displaying through me. Teach me, Lord, to love unconditionally because You always show that type of love toward me. Help me to understand that love is patient, kind, humble, and genuine. Without Your unconditional love, I would be without hope. Thank You, Lord, for loving me. Keep me with a heart filled with love. Show me how to think, talk, and react in a loving manner. May my words, thoughts, and actions be loving and show the importance of love. In Jesus' name, I pray. Amen!

 ### Monthly Challenge

Display the spirit of love by giving an inspirational note or card to three (3) people each week. God gave the greatest love gift you could ever receive – Jesus Christ. Practice showing the love of Christ wherever you go.

 ### Daily Checklist

Each day, answer the six questions. Once you have answered them, place a checkmark in the box on the Daily Checklist chart.

1. Did you pray today?
2. Did you read a scripture(s)?
3. Did you pray for someone? Who?
4. Did you fast today?
5. Did you witness to someone about Jesus?
6. What did you receive from the Lord today?

December ■ God's Gift of Love

DAILY CHECKLIST	Day 1	Day 2	Day 3	Day 4	Day 5	Day 6	Day 7
Week 1							
Week 2							
Week 3							
Week 4							
Week 5							

December 1: _____

_____

_____

December 2: _____

_____

_____

_____

December 3: _____

_____

_____

_____

December 4: _____

_____

_____

_____

December 5: _____

_____

_____

_____

Be BAD! Prayer Journal

December 6:

December 7:

December 8:

December 9:

December 10:

December 11:

December 12:

December 13:

December 14:

December 15:

December 16:

December 17:

December 18:

December 19:

December 20:

December 21:

December 22:

December 23:

December 24:

December 25:

December 26:

December 27:

December 28:

December 29:

Be BAD! Prayer Journal

December 30: _____

_____

_____

_____

December 31: _____

_____

_____

_____

DECEMBER—DAILY BIBLE READING

Date	Morning	Evening	✓
1	2 Peter 3	Ezekiel 40, 41	
2	1 John 1	Ezekiel 42, 43, 44	
3	1 John 2	Ezekiel 45, 46	
4	1 John 3	Ezekiel 47, 48	
5	1 John 4	Daniel 1, 2	
6	1 John 5	Daniel 3, 4	
7	2 John	Daniel 5, 6, 7	
8	3 John	Daniel 8, 9, 10	
9	Jude	Daniel 11, 12	
10	Revelation 1	Hosea 1, 2, 3, 4	
11	Revelation 2	Hosea 5, 6, 7, 8	
12	Revelation 3	Hosea 9, 10, 11	
13	Revelation 4	Hosea 12, 13, 14	
14	Revelation 5	Book of Joel	
15	Revelation 6	Amos 1, 2, 3	
16	Revelation 7	Amos 4, 5, 6	
17	Revelation 8	Amos 7, 8, 9	
18	Revelation 9	Book of Obadiah	
19	Revelation 10	Book of Jonah	
20	Revelation 11	Micah 1, 2, 3	
21	Revelation 12	Micah 4, 5	
22	Revelation 13	Micah 6, 7	
23	Revelation 14	Book of Nahum	
24	Revelation 15	Book of Habakkuk	
25	Revelation 16	Book of Zephaniah	
26	Revelation 17	Book of Haggai	
27	Revelation 18	Zechariah 1, 2, 3, 4	
28	Revelation 19	Zechariah 5, 6, 7, 8	
29	Revelation 20	Zechariah 9, 10, 11	
30	Revelation 21	Zechariah 12, 13, 14	
31	Revelation 22	Book of Malachi	

NOTES:

_____

_____

_____

_____

ANSWERED PRAYER

Prayer Request	Date of Request	Date Answered

Prayer Request	Date of Request	Date Answered

Prayer Request	Date of Request	Date Answered

www.ingramcontent.com/pod-product-compliance
Lightning Source LLC
LaVergne TN
LVHW061315060426
835507LV00019B/2160